Self-Awareness

Name _____

You are so special that your picture and name ____ e printed on a $1,000,000 bill. Draw and colo_____ urself in the circle. Write your first and last names on

Self-Awareness

Name _____

Write your birthday and age on the cake. Draw and color a picture of your birthday wish in the smoke puff.

I am ____ years old.

Self-Awareness

Name _____

Make a paper-bag puppet of yourself. Draw and color your face and hair on the head section below. Draw and color the clothes you most like to wear on the body section. Cut out the pieces. Glue the head to the bottom of a small paper bag. Glue the body to the bag below the head. Use the puppet to tell the class about yourself.

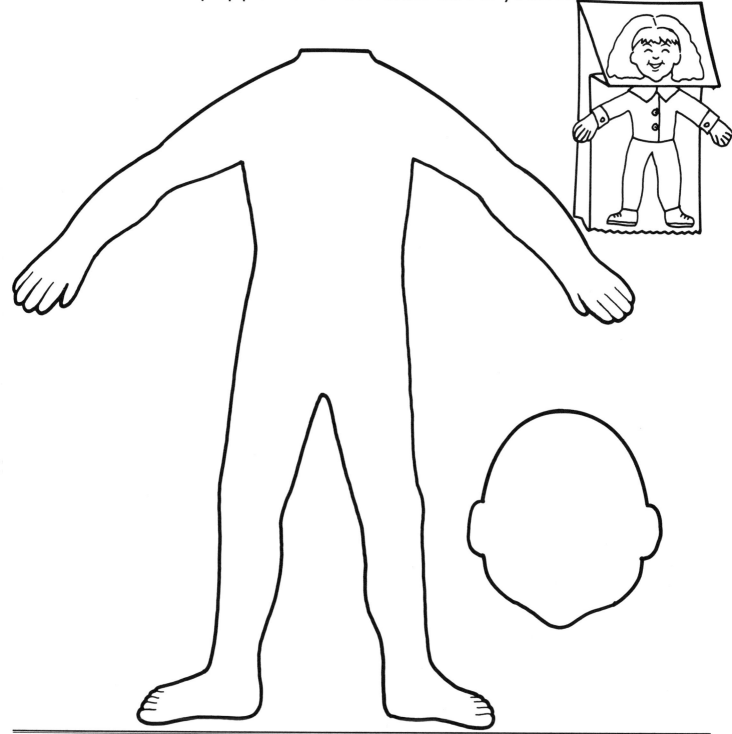

Self-Awareness

Name _____

Write your telephone number on the telephone. Practice dialing your telephone number.

Self-Awareness

Name _____

Write your address on the mailbox. Color the grass green and the flag red.

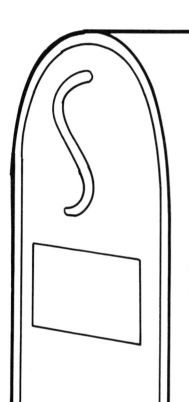

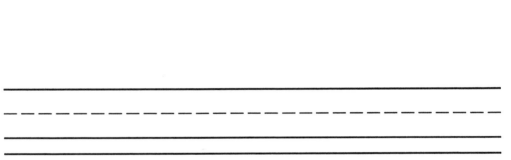

Self-Awareness

Name _____

Write the name of your favorite cereal on the box. Decorate the box. In the bowl, draw and color the cereal. Then draw and color the fruit that you like to eat on top of your cereal.

Self-Awareness

Name _____

Draw and color a picture of your pet or a pet you would like to have. Write the name of your pet on the carrier.

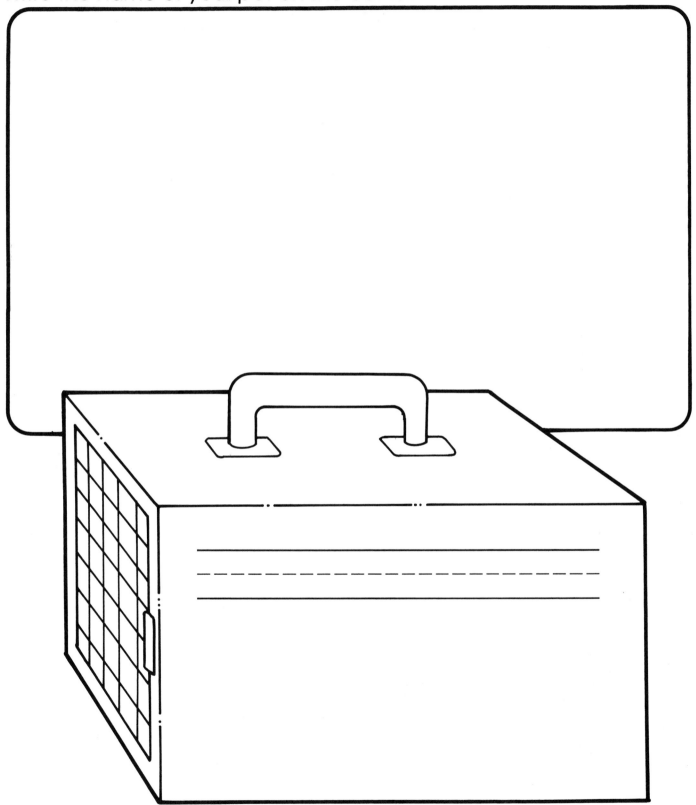

Self-Awareness

Name _____

Write the name of your favorite book. Decorate the cover.

Self-Awareness

Name _____

Think about objects you like to collect or make yourself. Draw and color a picture in the display case of the thing or things you collect or make.

Self-Awareness

Name _____

Draw and color a picture of your favorite place to go with your family. When you are finished, tell the class about a time you went to this place.

Language Arts

Name _____

Trace the dotted lines. Start at the left and go to the right.

Language Arts

Name _____

Trace the dotted lines. Start at the left and go to the right.

Language Arts

Name _____

Color the picture in each row that is the same as the first picture.

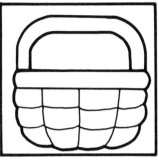   

 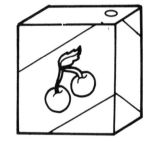  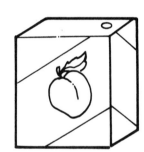

Language Arts

Name _____

Color the top picture. Add the missing parts to the bottom picture to make it look the same as the top picture. Color.

Language Arts

Name _____

Look at the animals in each row. Draw an **X** on the one that is different.

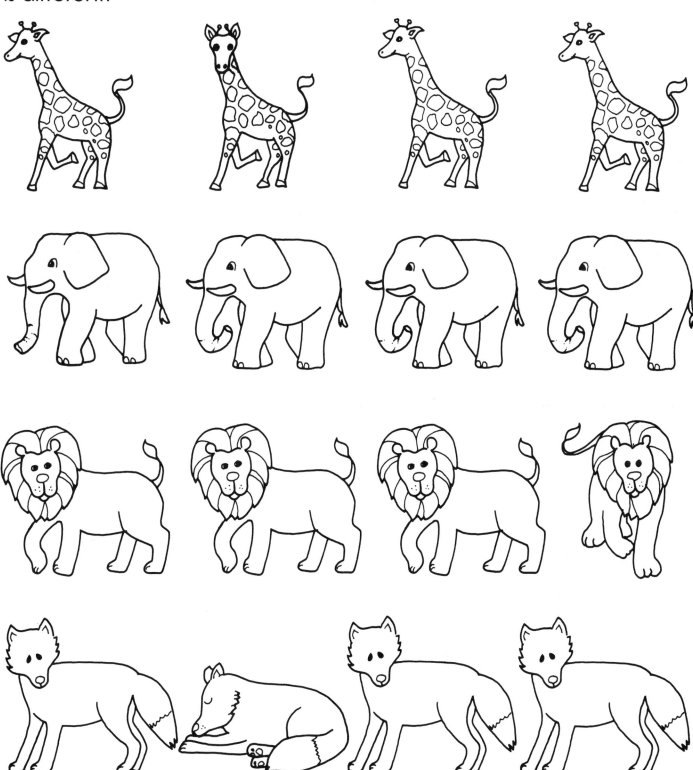

Language Arts

Name _____

Draw an **X** on six things in the bottom picture that are different from the top picture.

Language Arts

Name _____

Write the missing capital letters.

A ___ ___ D ___ ___ G

___ K ___ M ___ O ___ Q

S ___ U ___ W ___ Y ___

Write the alphabet in capital letters.

Language Arts

Name _____

Connect the dots in **ABC** order. Then color the picture.

Language Arts

Name _____

Write the missing lower-case letters.

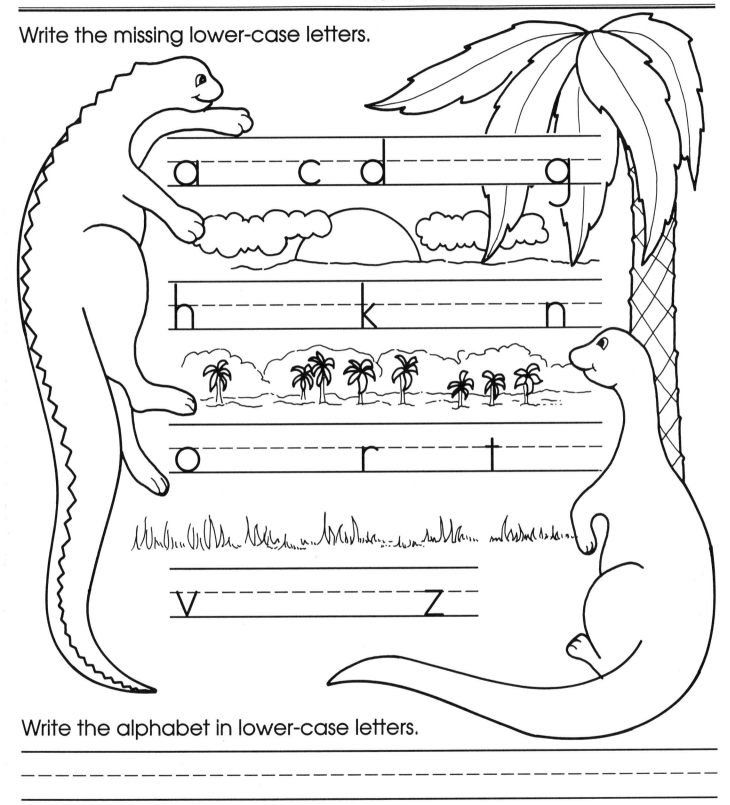

a ___ c d ___ ___ g

h ___ ___ k ___ n

o ___ r ___ t

v ___ z

Write the alphabet in lower-case letters.

_____

_____

_____

Language Arts

Name _____

Connect the dots in **abc** order. Then color the picture.

Language Arts

Name _____

Draw a line to match each capital letter with its correct lower-case letter.

C
G
B
K
E
M
J

g
m
e
c
j
b
k

H
L
A
F
I
D

a
i
h
d
l
f

Language Arts

Name _____

Draw a line to match each capital letter with its correct lower-case letter.

 R   v

 N   r

 Y   u

 V   x

 O   y

 X   o

U

 Z   w

 S   z

 P   t

 W   p

 Q   s

T   q

Language Arts

Name _____

Find Buster Beaver. If the picture begins with the sound of **B** ,
color the space brown. Color all other spaces blue.

Language Arts

Name _____

Help Cornelius Camel reach the candy store. Color only the pictures that begin with the sound of **C** 🥕

Candy Store

Language Arts

Name _____

Debbie Dinosaur eats delicious, decorated donuts all day long. Color only the pictures that begin with the sound of **D**

Language Arts

Name _____

All Franklin Fox ever dreams about is being a famous football player.
Put an **X** on only the pictures that begin with the sound of **F**

Language Arts

Name _____

Grady Goose gobbles gumdrops. Color only the pictures that begin with the sound of **G**

Language Arts

Name _____

Draw a line from Henrietta Hippo to each hotdog that has a picture beginning with the sound of **H** 🎩

Language Arts

Name _____

Help Jasper Jaguar find his jacket. Color only the pictures that begin with the sound of **J** 🫙

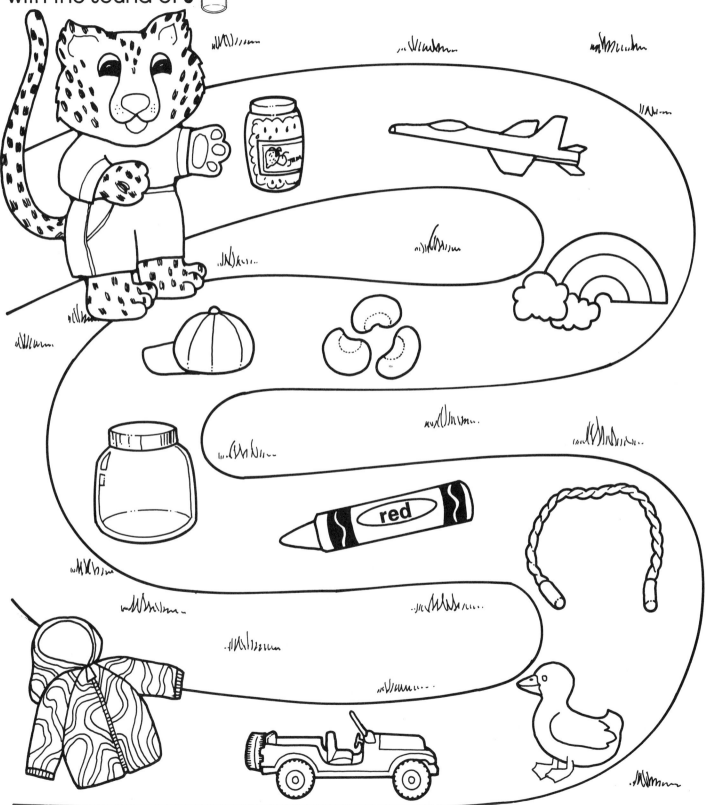

Language Arts

Name _____

Draw a line from King Kermit to each picture that begins with the sound of **K** 🐜🪁. Then color the pictures.

Language Arts

Name _____

If the picture begins with the sound of **L** , color the space yellow. Color all other spaces green to find Leo Lion.

Language Arts

Name _____

Help Mandi Mouse perform magic. Color only the pictures that begin with the sound of **M**

Language Arts

Name _____

If the picture begins with the sound of **N** , color the space black. Color all the other spaces yellow to find the musical notes.

Language Arts

Name _____

Peppy Patty eats popcorn all the time. Draw a piece of popcorn around each picture that begins with the sound of **P**

Language Arts

Name _____

Help Queen Quizzer reach her throne. Color only the pictures that begin with the sound of **Q** 👑

Language Arts

Name _____

Help Robert Rabbit pick the perfect raisins for his muffins. Draw a raisin around each picture that begins with the sound of **R**

Language Arts

Name _____

Sylvester makes sodas. He needs to know which scoops of ice cream he should use. Draw a line from the soda to each picture that begins with the sound of **S** ☆

Language Arts

Name _____

Help Tad Tiger decide which T-shirts to buy. Color only the T-shirts with pictures that begin with the sound of **T** 🚂

38

Language Arts

Name _____

Help Vanessa load violets in the van. Draw a line from the van to each picture that begins with the sound of **V**

Language Arts

Name _____

Wendy Walrus likes to make wishes. Color only the pictures that begin with the sound of **W**

Language Arts

Name _____

Yoshi Yak enjoys playing with a yo-yo. Draw a line from Yoshi to each picture beginning with the sound of **Y**

Language Arts

Name _____

Zep Zebra likes living in the zoo. Color each picture that begins with the sound of **Z**

Language Arts

Name _____

Say the name of each picture. Write the letter that makes the beginning sound.

b c d f g h j k l m n p q r s t v w y z

1. _____

2. _____

3. _____

4. _____

5. _____

6. _____

7. _____

8. _____

9. _____

10. _____

IF8782 Kindergarten in Review

Language Arts

Name _____

Say the name of each picture. Write the letter that makes the beginning sound.

b c d f g h j k l m n p q r s t v w y z

1. _____

2. _____

3. _____

4. _____

5. _____

6. _____

7. _____

8. _____

9. _____

10. _____

Language Arts

Name _____

Draw a line to match the rhyming pictures.

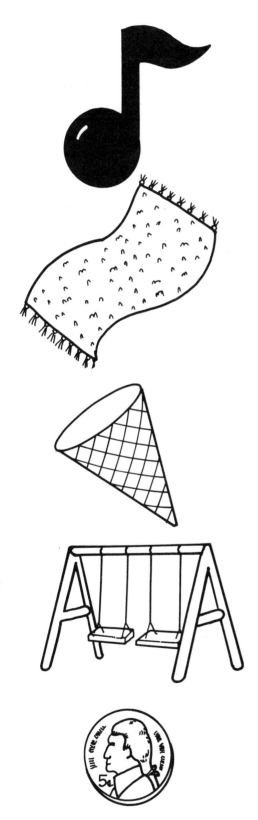
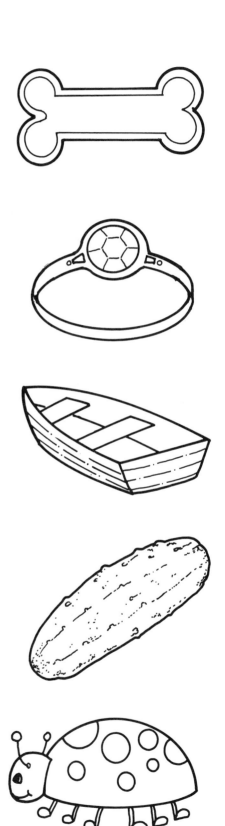

Language Arts

Name _____

Cut out the pictures at the bottom of this page. Paste each one in the box beside the picture that rhymes with it.

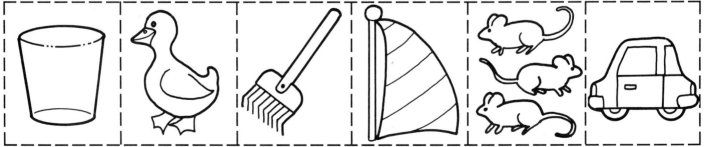

Language Arts

Name _____

Draw a line to match a picture with its opposite.

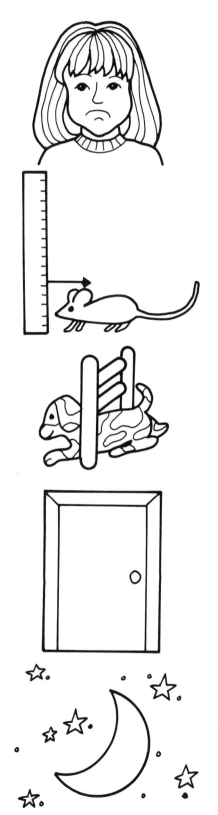

Language Arts

Name _____

Cut out the pictures at the bottom of the page. Paste each one in the circle beside the picture that means the opposite.

Language Arts

Name _____

Cut out the pictures at the bottom of the page. Paste them in the correct order.

1	2
3	4

Language Arts

Name _____

Write the numbers **1**, **2**, **3**, and **4** to show the correct order. Color the pictures.

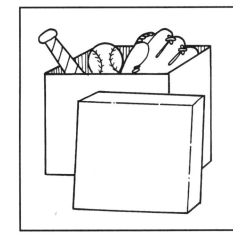

Look at the first picture in each row. Color the picture that shows what should happen next.

Ice Cream

single   50¢
double   75¢

Language Arts

Name _____

Look at the first picture in each row. Color the picture that shows what should happen next.

 IF8782 Kindergarten in Review

Math

Name _____

Cut out the pictures at the bottom of this page. Paste the pictures to continue the pattern in each row.

✂ --

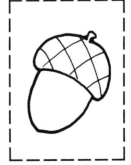

Math

Name _____

Draw the pictures to continue the pattern in each row.

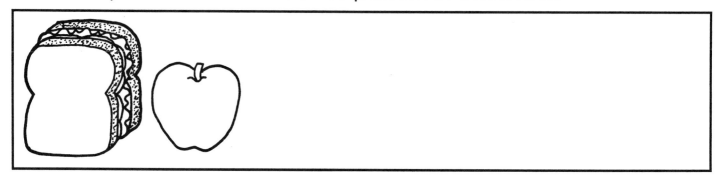

MATH

Name _____

Color the sea creatures the colors named. Then color the remaining creatures in each row to continue the pattern.

Starfish row: red, blue, _, _, _, _

Shells row: yellow, red, green, _, _, _

Fish row: red, red, blue, _, _, _

Seahorse row: red, green, red, blue, _, _, _, _

Math

Name _____

These were hungry kitties. Color the kitty bowls that have **0** food in them.

Practice writing the numeral **0**.

⌒ — — — — — — — — — — — — — — — —

Math

Name _____

Draw **1** sugar cube for each of Clay and Corky's horses.

Practice writing the numeral **1**.

- - - - - - - - - - - - - - - - - - - -

Math

Name _____

Help Seth and Samantha pack a picnic lunch. Color **2** of each item.

Practice writing the numeral **2**.

2 _____

Math

Name _____

Peanuts are elephants' favorite treats. Draw **3** peanuts  in each elephant's bag. Color the peanuts brown.

Practice writing the numeral **3**.

Math

Name _____

Casie Caterpillar enjoys blooming flowers. Draw a circle around each set of **4** flowers.

Practice writing the numeral **4**.

Math

Name _____

The cowhands are ready to saddle their horses. Color **5** horses in each corral.

Practice writing the numeral **5**.

Math

Name _____

Jasper, Jazelle and Jake Jaguar lost their beautiful spots. Draw **6** spots on each one. Color the spots black.

Practice writing the numeral **6**.

_____

Math

Name _____

Plucky Puffin eats fish for his dinner. Draw **7** fish for Plucky to catch. Color the fish yellow.

Practice writing the numeral **7**.

Math

Name _____

Ollie Owl watches the stars every night. Color **8** stars blue and **8** stars yellow.

Practice writing the numeral **8**.

Math

Name _____

Patsy Panda bought a beautiful new pencil for school. Draw **9** ♡ hearts and **9** ☆ stars on the pencil. Color the hearts ♡ red and the stars ☆ yellow.

Practice writing the numeral **9.**

Math

Name _____

Greta Goose has her own gumball machine. Color **10** gumballs red and **10** gumballs blue.

Practice writing the numeral **10**.

_____

Math

Name _____

Bethany Bear just loves berries. Draw **11** berries  on the bush. Color the berries purple.

Practice writing the numeral **11**.

Math

Name _____

Corky Crocodile loves to munch on cookies. Color **12** cookies for  Corky to munch.

Practice writing the numeral **12**.

12 -------------------------------------

Math

Name _____

Look at the picture of the Dinosaur Exhibit.

Tell how many you see. Write the number in the box.

Math

Name _____

Look at the picture of the pet store.

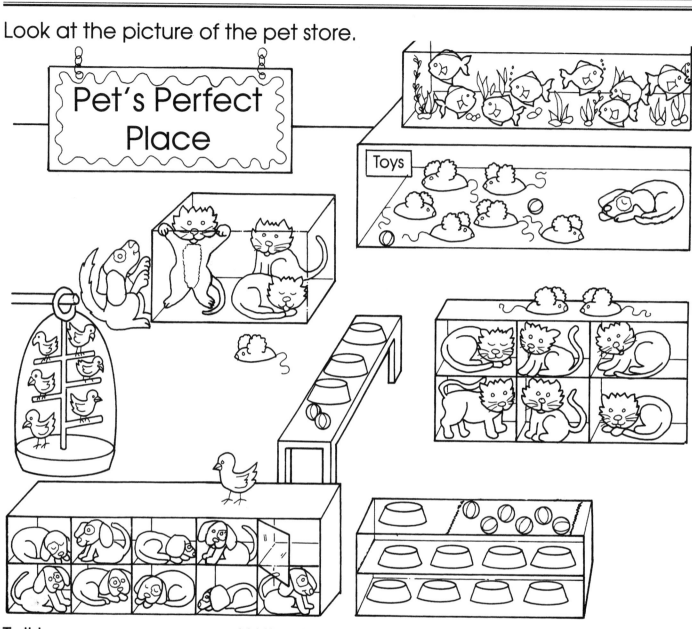

Pet's Perfect Place

Toys

Tell how many you see. Write the number in the box.

 ☐   ☐   ☐   ☐   ☐

 ☐   ☐   ☐   ☐

Math

Name _____

Write the missing numbers in each row.

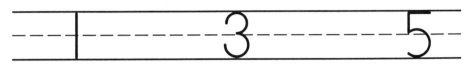

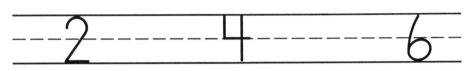

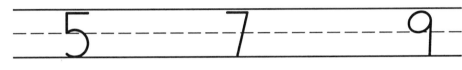

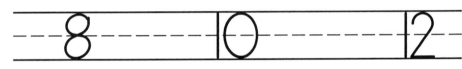

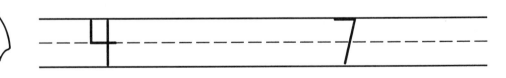

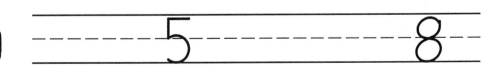

Math

Name _____

Draw a line to connect the dots in order starting with **1**. Then color the picture.

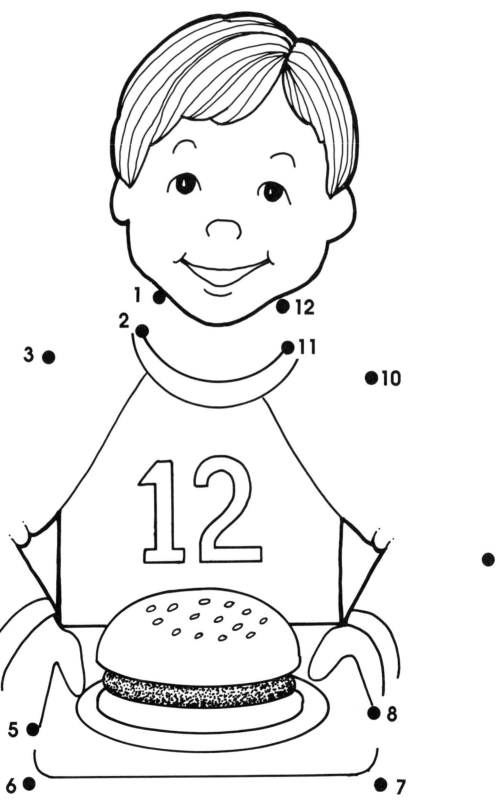

Math

Name _____

Look at the two pictures in each box. Color the picture that shows **more**.

Look at the two numbers in each box. Circle the number that is **more**.

4	6

5	3

9	7

12	10

0	2

8	1

Math

Name _____

Look at the two pictures in each box. Color the picture that shows **less**.

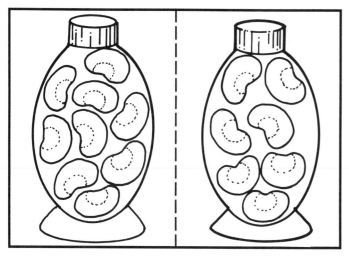

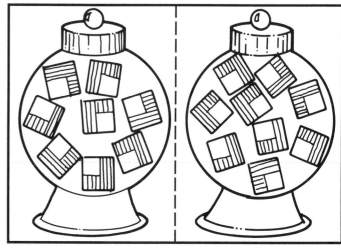

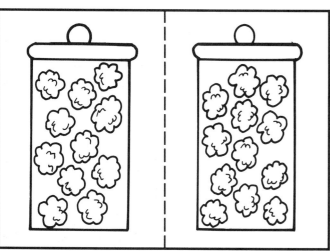

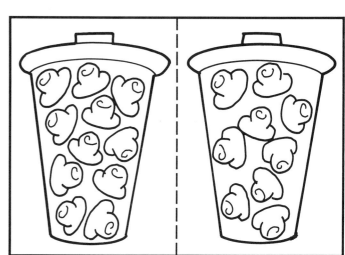

Look at the two numbers in each box. Circle the number that is **less**.

0	12

9	11

8	5

9	6

2	5

7	3

Math

Name _____

(Read the directions aloud as the children complete the picture.)

1. Draw a box around the **second** person in line.
2. Draw a line above the **fourth** person in line.
3. Draw an **X** on the **first** person in line.
4. Draw a line under the **fifth** person in line.
5. Circle the **third** person in line.

Math

Name _____

Color the hidden shapes using the following colors:

 gray   red   blue ⭐ yellow

Math

Name _____

Color the hidden shapes using the following colors:

△ green ⬭ blue ◯ gray ▭ brown

Social Studies

Name _____

Draw and color a picture in each locket frame. Cut out. Glue the tabs together.

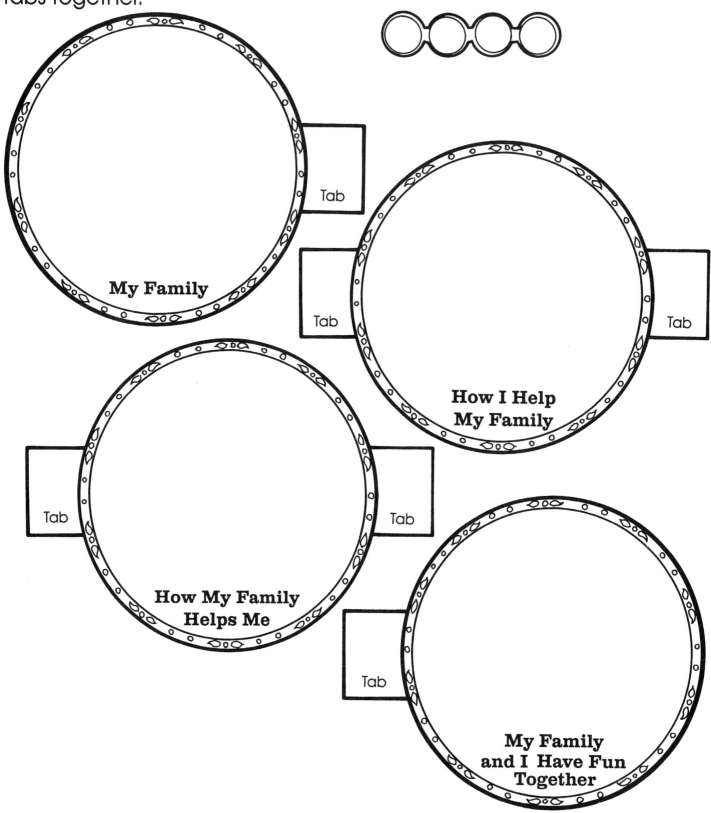

My Family

Tab

**How I Help
My Family**

Tab

Tab

**How My Family
Helps Me**

Tab

Tab

**My Family
and I Have Fun
Together**

Social Studies

Name _____

Color each picture that shows how family members help each other.

 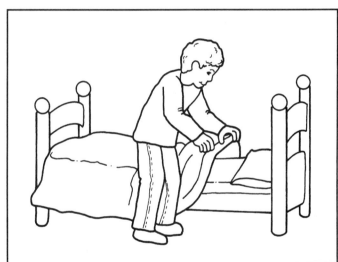

Social Studies

Name _____

Cut out the pictures at the bottom of the page. Paste the picture of each neighborhood helper in the box beside the job he or she does.

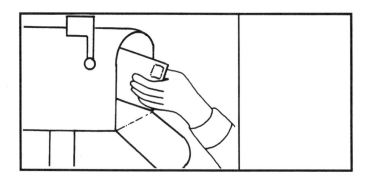

| doctor | police officer | mail carrier | librarian | baker | firefighter |

Social Studies

Name _____

Number the pictures in order.

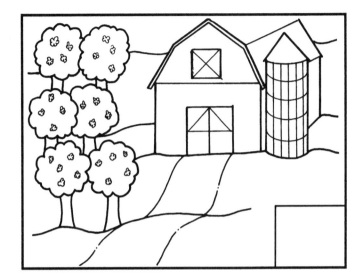

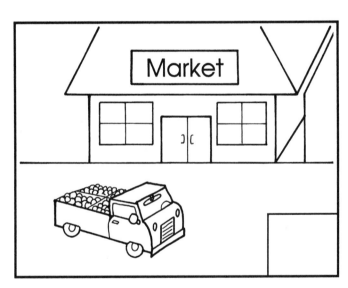

Draw and color a picture of your favorite fruit.

Social Studies

Name _____

Draw a line to match each farm crop to a product that is made from it.

Social Studies

Name _____

Draw each type of transportation where it belongs.

car   plane   train   boat

Social Studies

Name _____

Think about what you would like to do when you grow up. Draw and color the clothes you would wear while doing this job.

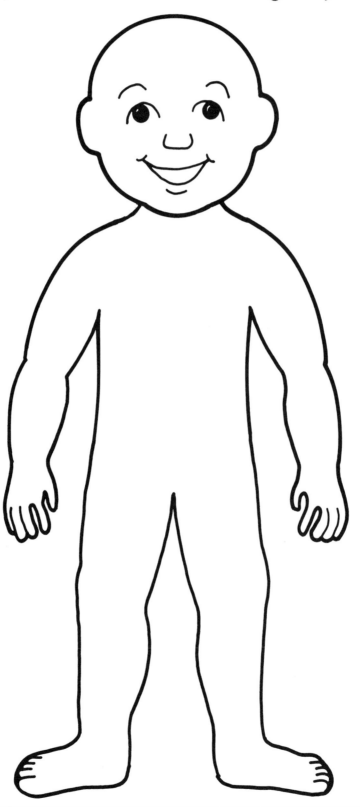

Science

Name _____

Cut out the pictures at the bottom of the page. Paste them over the numbers in the correct order.

1	2
3	4

✂ -

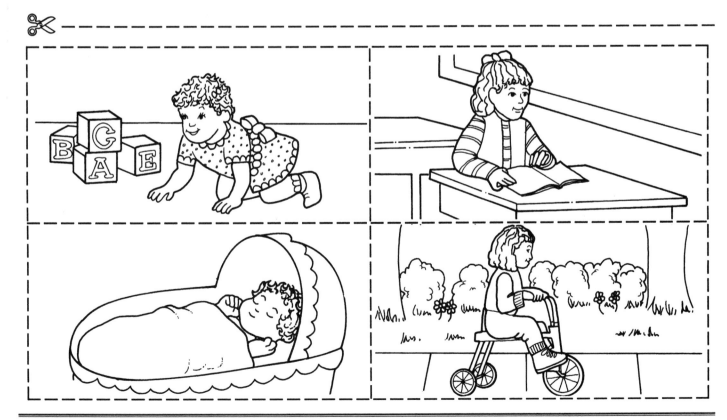

85   IF8782 Kindergarten in Review

Science

Name _____

Color the pictures of things you might ...

taste—red   touch—green   hear—orange

smell—yellow   see—blue

Science

Name _____

1. Draw a rake  in the picture of **fall**.

2. Draw a sled  in the picture of **winter**.

3. Draw a butterfly in the picture of **spring**.

4. Draw a swimming pool  in the picture of **summer**.

Science

Name _____

Draw a line from each weather picture to the clothes you should wear. Color the pictures.

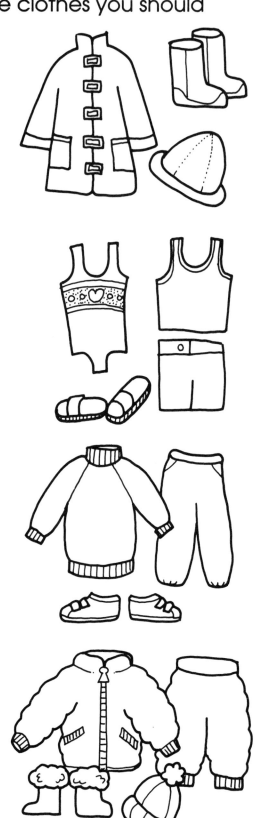

Science

Name _____

Look at the pictures. Draw a circle around each picture of a plant. Draw an **X** on each picture of an animal.

Science

Name _____

Cut out the animal pictures at the bottom of this page. Paste each picture where it belongs.

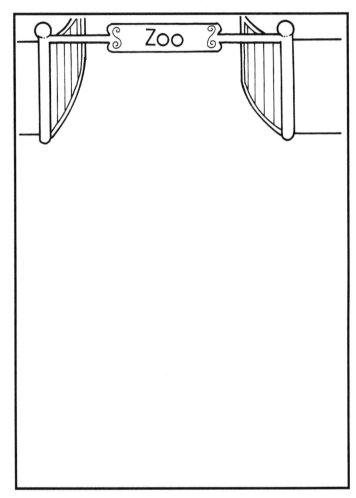

lion

horse

elephant

cow

zebra

giraffe

chicken

pig

monkey

sheep

Science

Name _____

Look at the pictures. Color the pictures of things that are solids **red**.
Color the liquids **blue** and the gases **yellow**.

Health

Circle each picture that shows how to take good care of your body.

Health

Name _____

Draw a face on the person in each picture to show how he or she might feel. Color the pictures.

 happy sad angry scared

Health

Name _____

Look at the face beside each mirror. Draw and color a picture in each mirror of what would make you feel that way.

sad

happy

scared

angry

Health

Name _____

Look at the pictures in each of the food groups in the pyramid.
Draw an **X** on the foods that do not belong in each group.

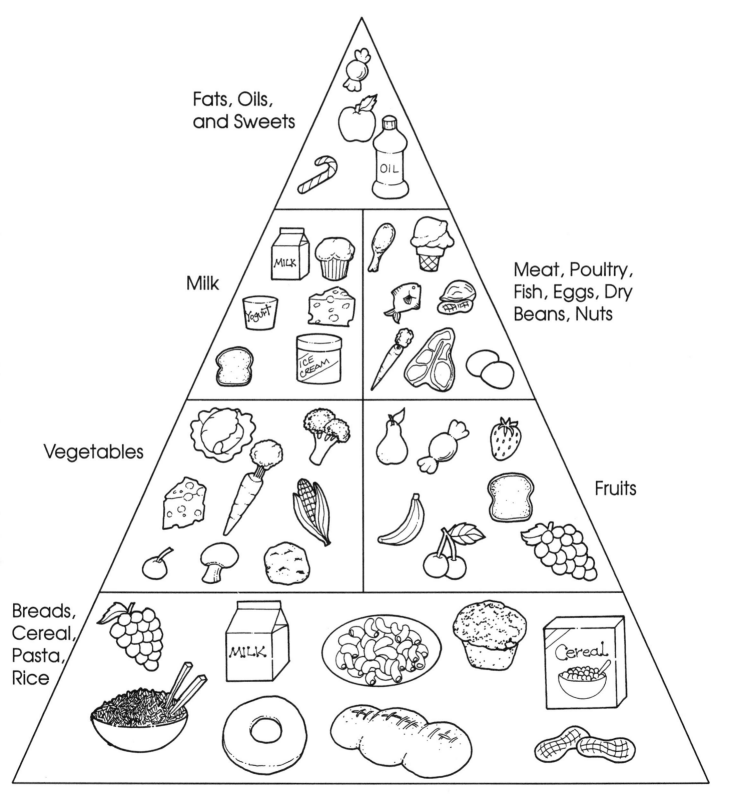

© Instructional Fair, Inc.

95

IF8782 Kindergarten in Review

Health

Name _____

Cut out the pictures at the bottom of the page. Look at the picture in each box. Paste the picture that shows what should happen next beside it.

 —

Health

Name _____

Look at the first picture in each row. Color the picture that shows what should happen next.

 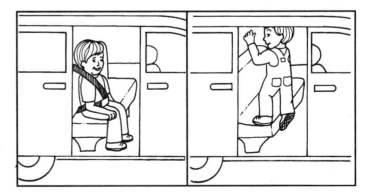

Listening and Following Directions

Name _____

(Read the directions aloud as the students complete the picture.)

1. Draw a hat **on** the rabbit's head. Color it brown.
2. Draw a haystack to the **left** of the rabbit. Color it yellow.
3. Draw four carrots **in** the wheelbarrow. Color them orange.
4. Draw a tree to the **right** of the rabbit.
5. Draw a sun **over** the haystack.
6. Draw grass **under** the wheelbarrow.

Now, finish coloring the picture.

Listening and Following Directions

Name _____

(Read the directions aloud as the students complete the picture.)

1. Draw a moon to the **right** of the lighthouse. Color it yellow.
2. Draw two fish to the **left** of the sailboat. Color them orange.
3. Draw a seashell **on** the sail of the boat.
4. Draw three stars **in** the sky.
5. Draw two flowers **in front of** the lighthouse. Color one pink and one purple.
6. Draw a starfish **in front of** the sailboat. Color it brown.

Now finish coloring the picture.

Colors

Name _____

Color each crayon the correct color. Draw a line from each crayon to the things that could be that color.

Colors

Name _____

Color each crayon the correct color. Then color each space in the picture the correct color.

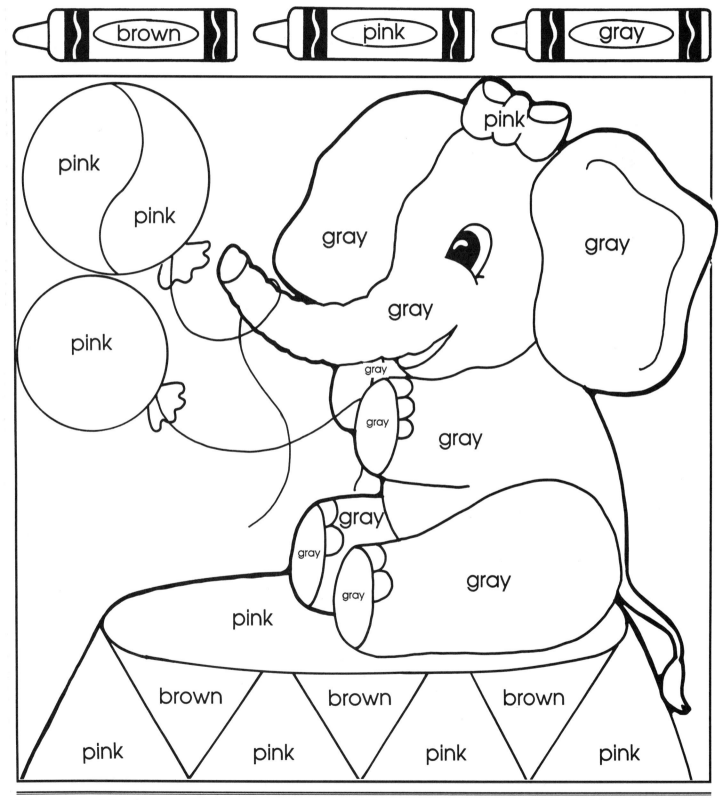

Colors

Name _____

Color each paintbrush the correct color. Then color each space in the picture the correct color.

white   black   green   blue   yellow

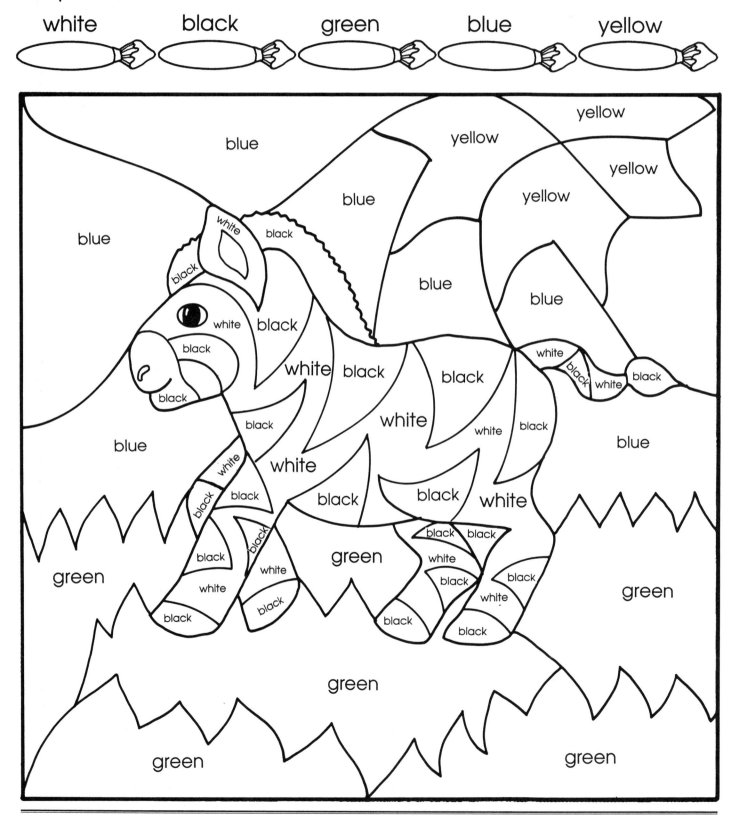

Answer Key
Kindergarten in Review

Self-Awareness   Name _____

You are so special that your picture and name are going to be printed on a $1,000,000 bill. Draw and color a picture of yourself in the circle. Write your first and last names on the lines.

$1,000,000 ﹏﹏﹏$1,000,000

Answers will vary.

$1,000,000 ﹏﹏﹏$1,000,000

Page 1

Self-Awareness   Name _____

Write your birthday and age on the cake. Draw and color a picture of your birthday wish in the smoke puff.

Pictures will vary

Answers will vary
I am ____ years old.

Page 2

Self-Awareness   Name _____

Write your telephone number on the telephone. Practice dialing your telephone number.

Answers will vary.

Page 4

Self-Awareness

Name _____

Write your address on the mailbox. Color the grass green and the flag red.

Answers will vary.

Page 5

Self-Awareness

Name _____

Write the name of your favorite cereal on the box. Decorate the box. In the bowl, draw and color the cereal. Then draw and color the fruit that you like to eat on top of your cereal.

Answers will vary.

Page 6

Self-Awareness

Name _____

Draw and color a picture of your pet or a pet you would like to have. Write the name of your pet on the carrier.

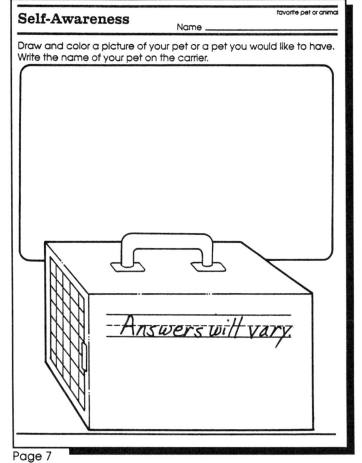

Answers will vary.

Page 7

Self-Awareness

Name _____

Write the name of your favorite book. Decorate the cover.

Answers will vary.

Page 8

Self-Awareness

Name _____

Think about objects you like to collect or make yourself. Draw and color a picture in the display case of the thing or things you collect or make.

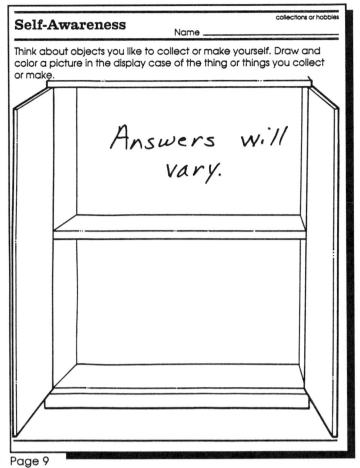

Answers will vary.

Page 9

Self-Awareness

Name _____

Draw and color a picture of your favorite place to go with your family. When you are finished, tell the class about a time you went to this place.

Pictures will vary.

Page 10

Language Arts

Name _____

Trace the dotted lines. Start at the left and go to the right.

Page 11

Language Arts

Name _____

Trace the dotted lines. Start at the left and go to the right.

Page 12

Language Arts

Name _____

Color the picture in each row that is the same as the first picture.

Page 13

Language Arts

Name _____

Color the top picture. Add the missing parts to the bottom picture to make it look the same as the top picture. Color.

Page 14

Language Arts

Name _____

Look at the animals in each row. Draw an **X** on the one that is different.

Page 15

Language Arts

Name _____

Draw an **X** on six things in the bottom picture that are different from the top picture.

Page 16

Language Arts

Name _____

Write the missing capital letters.

A B C D E F G H I

J K L M N O P Q R

S T U V W X Y Z

Write the alphabet in capital letters.

A B C D E F G H I J K L M
N O P Q R S T U V W X Y
Z

Page 17

Language Arts

Name _____

Connect the dots in **ABC** order. Then color the picture.

Page 18

Language Arts

Name _____

Write the missing lower-case letters.

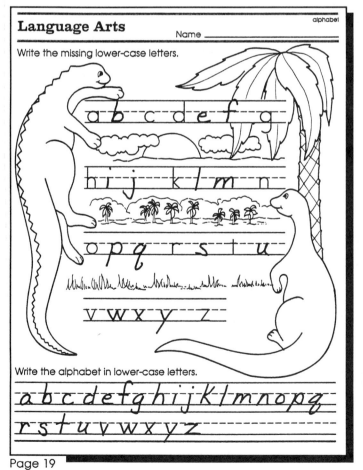

a b c d e f g

h i j k l m n

o p q r s t u

v w x y z

Write the alphabet in lower-case letters.

a b c d e f g h i j k l m n o p q
r s t u v w x y z

Page 19

Language Arts

Name _____

Connect the dots in **abc** order. Then color the picture.

Page 20

Draw a line to match each capital letter with its correct lower-case letter.

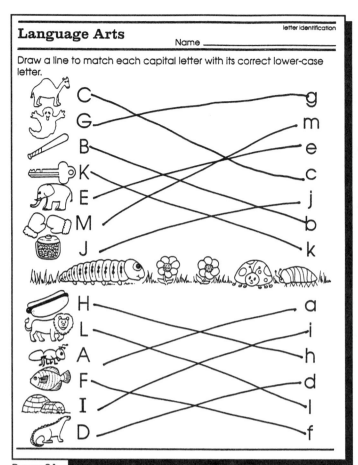

C
G
B
K
E
M
J

g
m
e
c
j
b
k

H
L
A
F
I
D

a
i
h
d
l
f

Draw a line to match each capital letter with its correct lower-case letter.

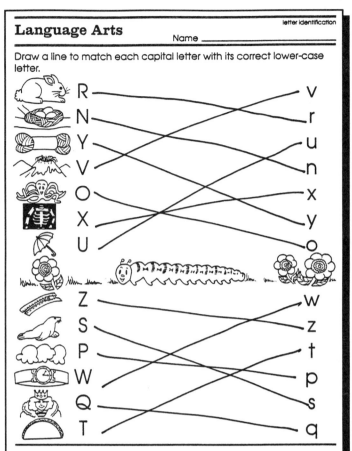

R
N
Y
V
O
X
U

v
r
u
n
x
y
o

Z
S
P
W
Q
T

w
z
t
p
s
q

Find Buster Beaver. If the picture begins with the sound of **B** color the space brown. Color all other spaces blue.

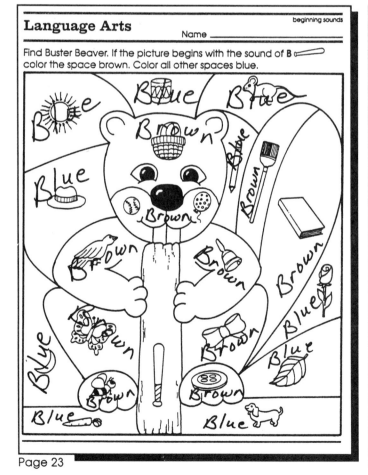

Help Cornelius Camel reach the candy store. Color only the pictures that begin with the sound of **C**

Language Arts

Name _____

Debbie Dinosaur eats delicious, decorated donuts all day long. Color only the pictures that begin with the sound of **D** 🍩

Page 25

Language Arts

Name _____

All Franklin Fox ever dreams about is being a famous football player. Put an **X** on only the pictures that begin with the sound of **F** 🪶

Page 26

Language Arts

Name _____

Grady Goose gobbles gumdrops. Color only the pictures that begin with the sound of **G** 🎁

Page 27

Language Arts

Name _____

Draw a line from Henrietta Hippo to each hotdog that has a picture beginning with the sound of **H** 🎩

Page 28

IF8782 Kindergarten in Review

Language Arts

Name _____

Help Jasper Jaguar find his jacket. Color only the pictures that begin with the sound of J

Page 29

Language Arts

Name _____

Draw a line from King Kermit to each picture that begins with the sound of K. Then color the pictures.

Page 30

Language Arts

Name _____

If the picture begins with the sound of L, color the space yellow. Color all other spaces green to find Leo Lion.

Page 31

Language Arts

Name _____

Help Mandi Mouse perform magic. Color only the pictures that begin with the sound of M

Page 32

Language Arts

Name _____

If the picture begins with the sound of **N** 🪆, color the space black. Color all the other spaces yellow to find the musical notes.

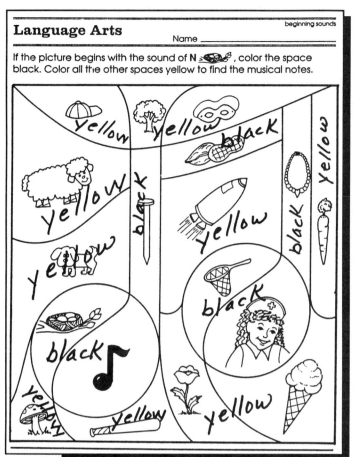

Page 33

Language Arts

Name _____

Peppy Patty eats popcorn all the time. Draw a piece of popcorn around each picture that begins with the sound of **P** ☁

Page 34

Language Arts

Name _____

Help Queen Quizzer reach her throne. Color only the pictures that begin with the sound of **Q** 👑

Page 35

Language Arts

Name _____

Help Robert Rabbit pick the perfect raisins for his muffins. Draw a raisin around each picture that begins with the sound of **R** 🐰

Page 36

Language Arts

Name _____

Sylvester makes sodas. He needs to know which scoops of ice cream he should use. Draw a line from the soda to each picture that begins with the sound of **S** ☆

Page 37

Language Arts

Name _____

Help Tad Tiger decide which T-shirts to buy. Color only the T-shirts with pictures that begin with the sound of **T**

Page 38

Language Arts

Name _____

Help Vanessa load violets in the van. Draw a line from the van to each picture that begins with the sound of **V**

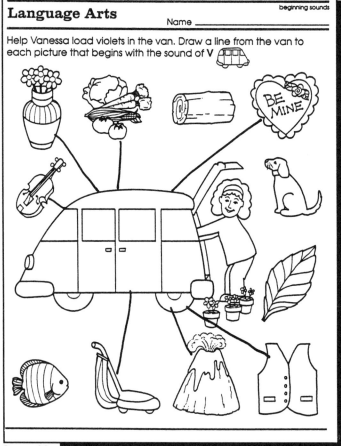

Page 39

Language Arts

Name _____

Wendy Walrus likes to make wishes. Color only the pictures that begin with the sound of **W**

Page 40

IF8782 Kindergarten in Review

Name _____

Yoshi Yak enjoys playing with a yo-yo. Draw a line from Yoshi to each picture beginning with the sound of **Y** 🧶

Page 41

Name _____

Zep Zebra likes living in the zoo. Color each picture that begins with the sound of **Z**

Page 42

Name _____

Say the name of each picture. Write the letter that makes the beginning sound.

b c d f g h j k l m n p q r s t v w y z

1. d
2. s
3. j
4. w
5. n
6. k
7. p
8. s
9. f
10. q

Page 43

Name _____

Say the name of each picture. Write the letter that makes the beginning sound.

b c d f g h j k l m n p q r s t v w y z

1. m
2. z
3. v
4. d
5. y
6. h
7. t
8. r
9. l
10. c

Page 44

Language Arts
Name _____

Draw a line to match the rhyming pictures.

Language Arts
Name _____

Cut out the pictures at the bottom of this page. Paste each one in the box beside the picture that rhymes with it.

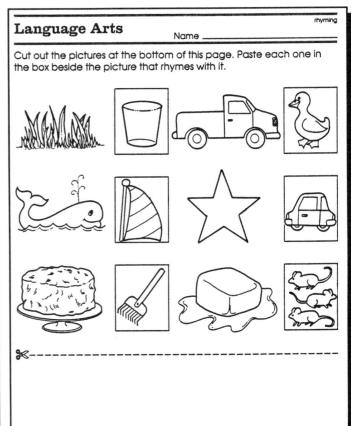

✂ — — — — — — — — — — — — — — — — — —

Language Arts
Name _____

Draw a line to match a picture with its opposite.

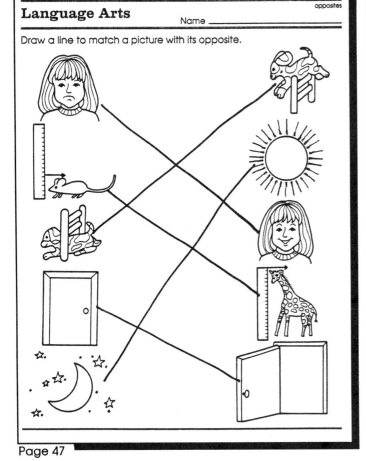

Language Arts
Name _____

Cut out the pictures at the bottom of the page. Paste each one in the circle beside the picture that means the opposite.

✂ — — — — — — — — — — — — — — — — — —

Language Arts

sequencing

Name _____

Write the numbers **1**, **2**, **3**, and **4** to show the correct order. Color the pictures.

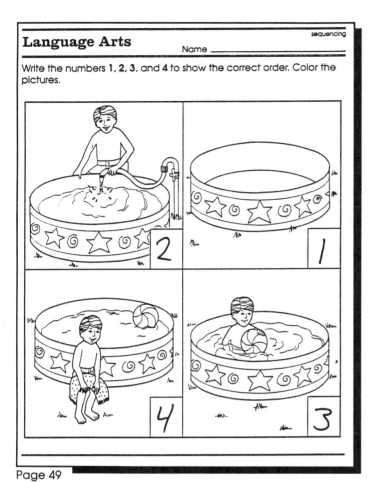

Language Arts

sequencing

Name _____

Cut out the pictures at the bottom of the page. Paste them in the correct order.

Language Arts

drawing conclusions

Name _____

Look at the first picture in each row. Color the picture that shows what should happen next.

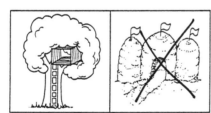

Language Arts

drawing conclusions

Name _____

Look at the first picture in each row. Color the picture that shows what should happen next.

IF8782 Kindergarten in Review

Math

Name _____

Cut out the pictures at the bottom of this page. Paste the pictures to continue the pattern in each row.

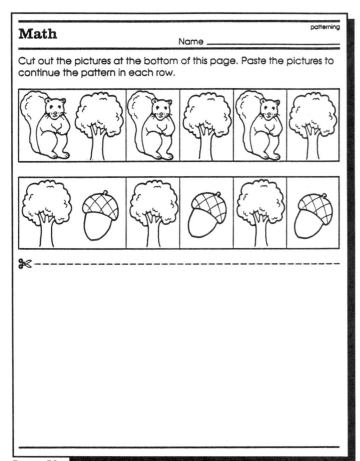

✂ -

Math

Name _____

Draw the pictures to continue the pattern in each row.

Math

Name _____

Color the sea creatures the colors named. Then color the remaining creatures in each row to continue the pattern.

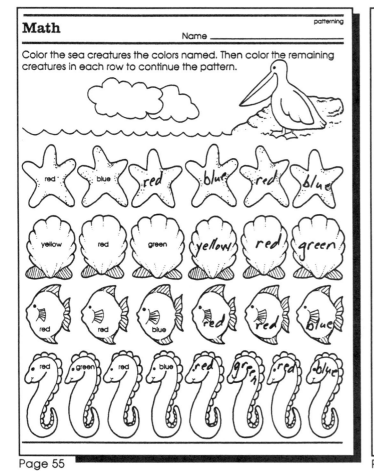

Math

Name _____

These were hungry kitties. Color the kitty bowls that have **0** food in them.

Practice writing the numeral **0**.

Math

Name _____

Draw **1** sugar cube  for each of Clay and Corky's horses.

Practice writing the numeral **1**.

_____

Math

Name _____

Help Seth and Samantha pack a picnic lunch. Color **2** of each item.

Practice writing the numeral **2**.

2 2 2 2 2 2 2 2 2 2 2 2

Math

Name _____

Peanuts are elephants' favorite treats. Draw **3** peanuts 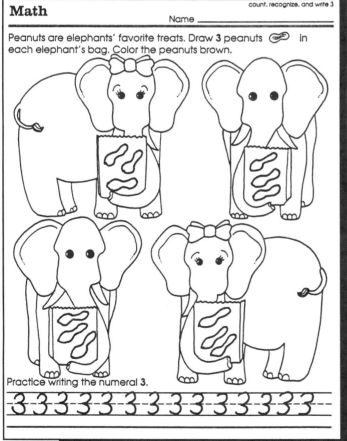 in each elephant's bag. Color the peanuts brown.

Practice writing the numeral **3**.

3 3 3 3 3 3 3 3 3 3 3 3 3 3

Math

Name _____

Casie Caterpillar enjoys blooming flowers. Draw a circle around each set of **4** flowers.

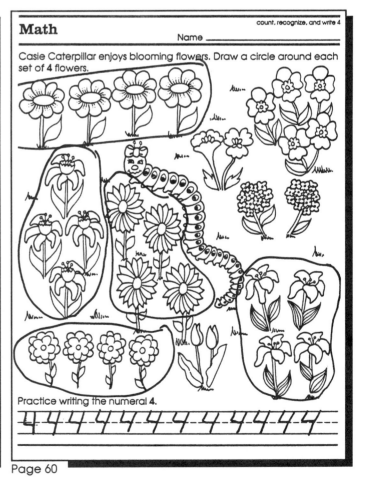

Practice writing the numeral **4**.

4 4 4 4 4 4 4 4 4 4 4

IF8782 Kindergarten in Review

Math

Name _____

The cowhands are ready to saddle their horses. Color **5** horses in each corral.

Practice writing the numeral **5**.

5 5 5 5 5 5 5 5 5 5 5 5

Math

Name _____

Jasper, Jazelle and Jake Jaguar lost their beautiful spots. Draw **6** spots on each one. Color the spots black.

Practice writing the numeral **6**.

6 6 6 6 6 6 6 6 6 6 6 6

Math

Name _____

Plucky Puffin eats fish for his dinner. Draw **7** fish for Plucky to catch. Color the fish yellow.

Practice writing the numeral **7**.

7 7 7 7 7 7 7 7 7 7 7 7

Math

Name _____

Ollie Owl watches the stars every night. Color **8** stars blue and **8** stars yellow.

Practice writing the numeral **8**.

8 8 8 8 8 8 8 8 8 8 8 8 8

IF8782 Kindergarten in Review

Math

Name _____

Patsy Panda bought a beautiful new pencil for school. Draw **9** ♡ hearts and **9** ☆ stars on the pencil. Color the hearts ♡ red and the stars ☆ yellow.

Practice writing the numeral **9**.

9 9 9 9 9 9 9 9 9 9 9 9 9

Page 65

Math

Name _____

Greta Goose has her own gumball machine. Color **10** gumballs red and **10** gumballs blue.

Practice writing the numeral **10**.

10 10 10 10 10 10 10 10 10

Page 66

Math

Name _____

Bethany Bear just loves berries. Draw **11** berries 🫐 on the bush. Color the berries purple.

Practice writing the numeral **11**.

11 11 11 11 11 11 11 11 11

Page 67

Math

Name _____

Corky Crocodile loves to munch on cookies. Color **12** cookies 🍪 for Corky to munch.

Practice writing the numeral **12**.

12 12 12 12 12 12 12

Page 68

Math

Name _____

Look at the picture of the Dinosaur Exhibit.

Tell how many you see. Write the number in the box.

| | 6 | | 3 | | 0 |
| 4 | | 2 | | 1 |

Math

Name _____

Look at the picture of the pet store.

Pet's Perfect Place

Toys

Tell how many you see. Write the number in the box.

| | 9 | | 10 | | 12 | | 8 |
| | 7 | | 11 | | 9 |

Math

Name _____

Write the missing numbers in each row.

Burger 99¢
Fries 50¢
Shake 89¢

1 2 3 4 5
2 3 4 5 6
5 6 7 8 9
8 9 10 11 12
7 8 9 10 11
4 5 6 7 8
4 5 6 7 8
2 3 4 5 6

Math

Name _____

Draw a line to connect the dots in order starting with 1. Then color the picture.

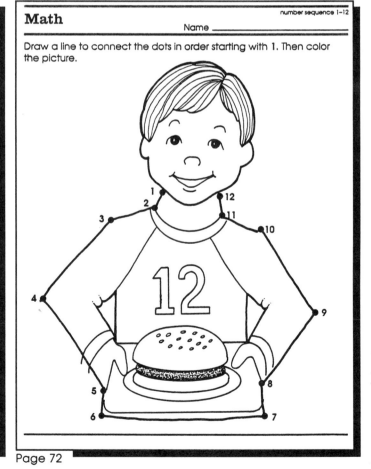

Math

Name _____

Look at the two pictures in each box. Color the picture that shows **more**.

Look at the two numbers in each box. Circle the number that is **more**.

Page 73

Math

Name _____

Look at the two pictures in each box. Color the picture that shows **less**.

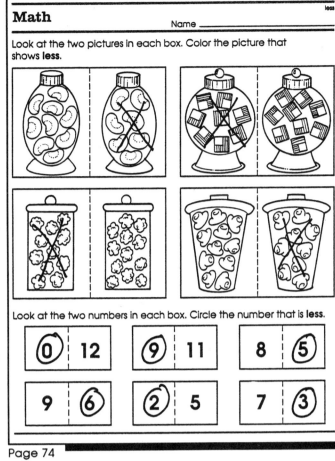

Look at the two numbers in each box. Circle the number that is **less**.

Page 74

Math

ordinal numbers

Name _____

(Read the directions aloud as the children complete the picture.)

1. Draw a box around the **second** person in line.
2. Draw a line above the **fourth** person in line.
3. Draw an **X** on the **first** person in line.
4. Draw a line under the **fifth** person in line.
5. Circle the **third** person in line.

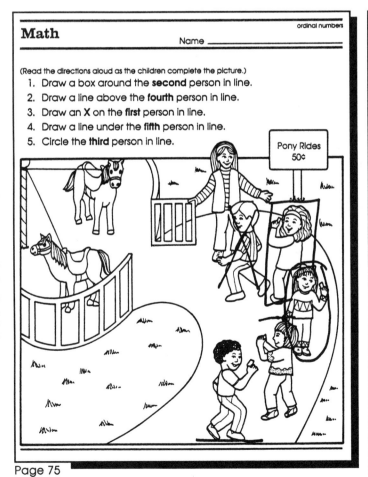

Page 75

Math

shapes

Name _____

Color the hidden shapes using the following colors:

gray   red   blue   yellow

Page 76

© Instructional Fair, Inc.   121   IF8782 Kindergarten in Review

Math

Name _____

Color the hidden shapes using the following colors:

△ green   ⬭ blue   ◯ gray   ▭ brown

Social Studies

Name _____

Draw and color a picture in each locket frame. Cut out. Glue the tabs together.

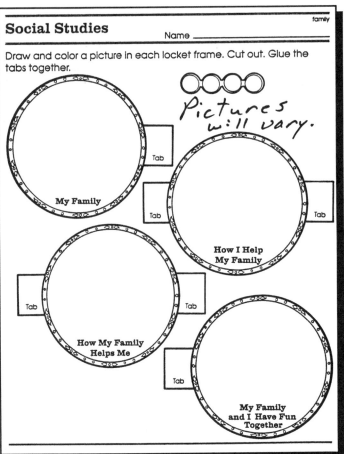

Pictures will vary.

My Family

Tab

How I Help My Family

Tab

Tab

How My Family Helps Me

Tab

Tab

My Family and I Have Fun Together

Social Studies

Name _____

Color each picture that shows how family members help each other.

Social Studies

Name _____

Cut out the pictures at the bottom of the page. Paste the picture of each neighborhood helper in the box beside the job he or she does.

mail carrier   police officer

librarian   doctor

baker   firefighter

       IF8782 Kindergarten in Review

Number the pictures in order.

Draw and color a picture of your favorite fruit.

Pictures will vary

Draw a line to match each farm crop to a product that is made from it.

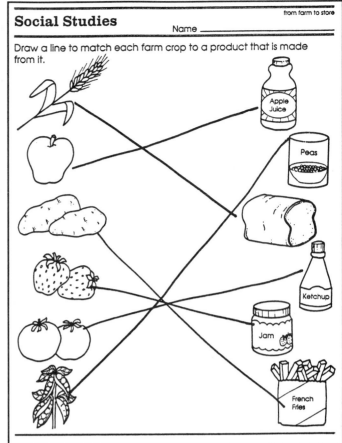

Draw each type of transportation where it belongs.

Think about what you would like to do when you grow up. Draw and color the clothes you would wear while doing this job.

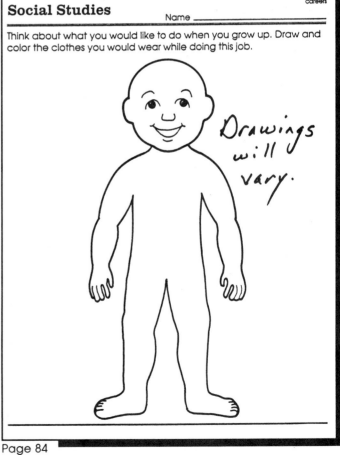

Drawings will vary.

Science

Name _____

Cut out the pictures at the bottom of the page. Paste them over the numbers in the correct order.

✂ -

Science

Name _____

Color the pictures of things you might ...

taste—red   hear—orange
smell—yellow   touch—green   see—blue

Answers may vary.

Science

Name _____

1. Draw a rake in the picture of **fall**.
2. Draw a sled in the picture of **winter**.
3. Draw a butterfly in the picture of **spring**.
4. Draw a swimming pool in the picture of **summer**.

Science

Name _____

Draw a line from each weather picture to the clothes you should wear. Color the pictures.

Science

Name _____

Look at the pictures. Draw a circle around each picture of a plant.
Draw an **X** on each picture of an animal.

Page 89

Science

Name _____

Cut out the animal pictures at the bottom of this page. Paste each
picture where it belongs.

Zoo

chicken   horse
sheep
pig   cow

giraffe
lion   zebra
elephant   monkey

Page 90

Science

Name _____

Look at the pictures. Color the pictures of things that are solids **red**.
Color the liquids **blue** and the gases **yellow**.

Page 91

Health

Name _____

Circle each picture that shows how to take good care of your body.

Page 92

Health

feelings

Name _____

Draw a face on the person in each picture to show how he or she might feel. Color the pictures.

😊 happy 😢 sad 😠 angry 😮 scared

Health

feelings

Name _____

Look at the face beside each mirror. Draw and color a picture in each mirror of what would make you feel that way.

Pictures will vary.

sad

happy

scared

angry

Health

food pyramid

Name _____

Look at the pictures in each of the food groups in the pyramid. Draw an **X** on the foods that do not belong in each group.

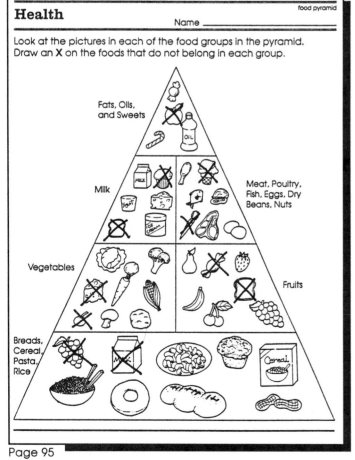

Fats, Oils, and Sweets

Milk

Meat, Poultry, Fish, Eggs, Dry Beans, Nuts

Vegetables

Fruits

Breads, Cereal, Pasta, Rice

Health

safety

Name _____

Cut out the pictures at the bottom of the page. Look at the picture in each box. Paste the picture that shows what should happen next beside it.

Health

Name _____

Look at the first picture in each row. Color the picture that shows what should happen next.

Listening and Following Directions

Name _____

(Read the directions aloud as the students complete the picture.)

1. Draw a hat **on** the rabbit's head. Color it brown.
2. Draw a haystack to the **left** of the rabbit. Color it yellow.
3. Draw four carrots **in** the wheelbarrow. Color them orange.
4. Draw a tree to the **right** of the rabbit.
5. Draw a sun **over** the haystack.
6. Draw grass **under** the wheelbarrow.

Now, finish coloring the picture.

Listening and Following Directions

Name _____

(Read the directions aloud as the students complete the picture.)

1. Draw a moon to the **right** of the lighthouse. Color it yellow.
2. Draw two fish to the **left** of the sailboat. Color them orange.
3. Draw a seashell **on** the sail of the boat.
4. Draw three stars **in** the sky.
5. Draw two flowers **in front of** the lighthouse. Color one pink and one purple.
6. Draw a starfish **in front of** the sailboat. Color it brown.

Now finish coloring the picture.

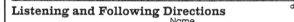

Colors

Name _____

Color each crayon the correct color. Draw a line from each crayon to the things that could be that color.

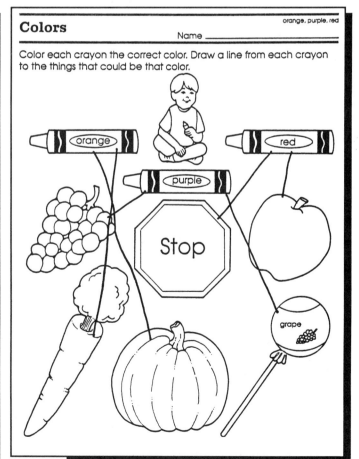

orange

red

purple

Stop

grape